This Book Belongs to:
MAGIC
MAGIC
MAGIC

BE WELL SPELLS
TISSUE
Cough & COLD

MAKEUP
XXX

MAGIC
DUST

SWEET

SPOOKY ST.

FLY ME
TO THE
MOON

MAGIC
HOCUS
POCUS
SPELLS
coffee

ZEN
witch

MAGIC 101
POISON
BAT BLOOD

TOAD
WARTS

PEOPLE I WANT TO SLAP
Leave me alone!

Thank you for purchasing this coloring book, one of many in the Chubby Mermaid series. Please don't forget to sign into Amzon.com – Deborah Muller Coloring Books and leave a review.

Follow me on Facebook
Chubby Mermaid Art by Deborah Muller

Join my Coloring Group on Facebook
Deborah Muller's Coloring Group

Instagram
Chubby Mermaid Art

Etsy
Chubby Mermaid

Pinterest
Deborah Muller Chubby Mermaid Art

Email
Chubbymermaid@hotmail.com

Website
ChubbyMermaidArt.com

Made in the USA
Columbia, SC
15 December 2024

49468817R00039